Original title:
Pine-Scented Prose

Copyright © 2025 Creative Arts Management OÜ
All rights reserved.

Author: Miriam Kensington
ISBN HARDBACK: 978-1-80566-776-6
ISBN PAPERBACK: 978-1-80566-796-4

The Smell of Serenity

In a forest where the trees all sway,
A squirrel sneezed and ran away.
The pine cones rolled in perfect rows,
As if they'd planned this little show.

The air was thick with scents so bold,
Like cookies fresh and stories told.
A deer slipped by, trying not to trip,
On her own two feet, she took a dip.

Treetop Tales

Up high where the birds like to sing,
A raccoon donned a shiny ring.
He thought it made him look so cool,
Till he fell in the pond — oh, what a fool!

A wise old owl gave advice so clear,
"Never wear bling when you're near here!"
And all the critters laughed with glee,
In this treetop world of pure jubilee.

Whispers of the Evergreen

The trees were gossiping, oh so loud,
About a bear who had been too proud.
He tried a dance but stepped on a root,
His big furry form could not compute!

The wind carried laughter through the leaves,
As blushing flowers hid beneath their sleeves.
A breeze tickled a chipmunk's cheek,
And soon they all joined in, quite the clique!

The Forest's Embrace

In the woods where shadows play,
A hedgehog rolled the night away.
He whispered secrets to the ground,
While mushrooms giggled all around.

The moon peeked through, casting a grin,
As the fireflies danced and spun.
With every flicker, a joke was told,
In the nighttime warmth, cozy and bold.

Beneath the Canopy

Under the trees, the squirrels do prance,
They dance in circles, they take a chance.
With acorn hats and berry-blue shoes,
They giggle and plot, crafting their ruse.

A raccoon peeks from behind the bark,
To join the fun, he brings a spark.
His stash of snacks, a sugary feast,\nNow the woodland's wild parties released.

Timbered Tales

Once there was a tree named Fred,
He dreamed of skies, but feared his bed.
He'd toss and turn in the thunder's might,
"Just let me swing with the birds in flight!"

A wise old owl laughed, fluffed his wing,
"Dear Fred, life's more fun than just to cling!
So up you go, let the winds prevail,
You'll find your voice in the forest tale."

Breezes Among the Boughs

The breezes whisper, tales unfold,
Of all the secrets the branches hold.
A rabbit hops in a little tutu,
Wiggling its tail, a curious view!

A fox rolls by with a comical grin,
"Who knew frolics could come with a spin?"
They play jump rope with the vine's embrace,
Laughter erupts in this woodland place.

Evergreen Echoes

Echoes of laughter among the trees,
From giggling critters who dance with ease.
A hedgehog spins in a bright red hat,
"Look at me go!" he shouts with a spat.

While chipmunks cheer with popcorn in tow,
They scatter and scatter, all in a row.
Beneath the dappled light they enjoy,
A festival of fun, every girl and boy.

Essence of the Woodlands

In the forest where trees stand tall,
Squirrels dance and acorns fall.
Bears do yoga in the sun,
Laughing at life's morning run.

Mice in sweaters sip hot tea,
Chasing shadows, wild and free.
A fox in bowtie leads the show,
Telling tales of twirling snow.

Sprucetide Stories

Under branches, tales unfold,
Of critters brave and hearts so bold.
Rabbits wear hats, looking dapper,
As they hop with a laugh, what a caper!

Chipmunks juggle while birds sing tunes,
Giggling softly under the moon.
Every whisper, a punchline found,
In this funny circus, joy abounds.

The Fragrance of Wilderness

In the wild, the air is rich,
With giggles and a little glitch.
A deer with glasses reads a book,
While crickets give their finest look.

The breeze carries a scent so sweet,
Of wildflower pie for a treat.
Bees buzz around, full of cheer,
They throw a party every year.

A Grove of Memories

Whispers of laughter in the air,
Trees gossip without a care.
An owl, the teacher, wise and spry,
Comments on the squirrels that fly by.

Badgers play chess, quite the sight,
While raccoons steal cookies at night.
In this grove, the humor's grand,
Nature's laughter, hand in hand.

Serenity of the Spruce

In the forest, the trees swap tales,
Of squirrel heists and windy gales.
A chipmunk chuckles at a wise old pine,
'You think you're tall? Your jokes are a sign!'

The birds gossip in their own little way,
'The rush of the world? We've no need to play.'
With each gentle breeze, laughter takes flight,
Whispering secrets till the stars shine bright.

What the Pines Remember

Ancient trunks with stories to tell,
Of wobbly branches where raccoons fell.
They giggle about acorn maps gone astray,
And how squirrels dance, 'til they tumble away!

The wind carries voices from long ago,
Of woodland parties where fungi grow.
Each ring in the bark, a punchline on hold,
Making the forest a comedy gold.

A Tangle of Roots

Underneath the surface, roots intertwine,
Holding hands with the fungi, what a twist divine!
They share a joke that makes the soil quake,
'Life's just like us, it's a give and take!'

With each silly knot and each loop of glee,
They tug and they pull, a wild jamboree.
A dance of laughter, deep in the ground,
Where only the critters can hear the sound.

Ink on the Forest Floor

A painter spills laughter on leaves so bold,
As colors of autumn begin to unfold.
Each brushstroke whispers a funny old joke,
'The best art takes time, just like a smoke!'

The forest floor's scribbles, whimsical sights,
Compose a scrap of hilarious insights.
With twigs as the quills and moss as the ink,
Nature's own humor makes us stop and think.

The Quiet of the Woodlands

In the woods where the squirrels dance,
With acorns poised, they take their chance.
Whispers of leaves, in jest they sway,
Nature's giggles guide the way.

Mushrooms prance in a dappled light,
With hats too big, it's quite the sight.
Frogs in tuxedos croak a tune,
While bees wear stripes beneath the moon.

A turtle slow, with wisdom vast,
Claims he's the fastest in the past.
But as he sips his morning tea,
A rabbit zooms past, wild and free.

Chipmunks bicker over nuts and treats,
While owls hoot puns as night retreats.
In woodlands quiet, laughter sings,
Amid the chirps and fluttering wings.

Notes from the Nature's Heart

Bubbles of laughter from a brook so clear,
With rocks as chairs, all creatures near.
A raccoon juggles berries with flair,
While ladybugs pause to catch the air.

The trees lean in, with gossip to share,
About the foxes, and their last affair.
A chorus of crickets hums along,
As fireflies twinkle to nature's song.

Grasshoppers cheer for the foolish worms,
Who think they can dance with all their turns.
In this garden of jest, wildflowers bloom,
As sunbeams kick up a golden plume.

Every rustle and chirp is welcomed here,
With chuckles abound from far and near.
Summer's tale unfolds, a merry play,
In nature's hall, where mirth holds sway.

Sylvan Stories

A bear on a tricycle rolls down the lane,
While birds share secrets, in sweet refrain.
A moose with glasses reads a tall tale,
While whispers of whimsy fill the gale.

The raccoon chef, with his paws in the dough,
Bakes cookies to share with a friendly crow.
But sprinkles fly high, a sweet confetti,
And all of a sudden, the squirrel's unsteady.

Ferns sway lightly, in soft summer air,
While bugs retell dramas, with flair and despair.
The trees roll their eyes at the gossip they hear,
"Oh, not again!" they murmur in cheer.

At twilight's edge, as the moon takes her throne,
Fireflies gather to dance, all alone.
With nature's laughter echoing wide,
In sylvan stories, we find joy inside.

Unfolding Under the Skies

In fields of green, where the daisies tease,
A pup runs wild, catching the breeze.
With floppy ears and a wagging tail,
He leads the birds in a raucous trail.

Clouds play hide and seek with the sun,
While rabbits race, just for fun.
The shadows stretch as jokes are exchanged,
In the lighthearted moments, all is arranged.

A turtle strums on a leaf-made lute,
As crickets tap dance in sequined suit.
Each blade of grass chuckles with mirth,
Spreading joy through the earth's embrace, its girth.

As twilight drapes her cozy shawl,
Fireflies gather, they're having a ball.
In secret laughter, the stars ignite,
Under vast skies, all feels just right.

Scent of Solitude

In the forest I trekked alone,
Lost my way, my phone's outgrown.
Trees chuckled as I passed them by,
Whispering secrets, oh me, oh my.

A squirrel waved with a tiny paw,
I laughed so hard, nearly saw my jaw.
The ferns rolled their leaves in delight,
Nature's giggles under moonlight.

Needles and Ink

With a pen in hand, I scribble my thought,
On a patch of bark where others are caught.
Each line a branch that twists and bends,
My ink flows like sap, where the laughter ends.

A deer peeped in, curious and sly,
Wondering why this silly man cries.
I told him tales of misty lakes,
He grinned and said, 'For goodness' sakes!'

In the Heart of the Woods

In the heart of the woods, a party's underway,
With owls and foxes, they dance and sway.
A raccoon DJ spins a funky beat,
While the beetles join in, tapping their feet.

The trees swayed too, in a rhythmic groove,
Nature's own moves, it's hard not to prove.
With laughter echoing through every bough,
Say cheese! The birds took a selfie, wow!

Aromas of the Wild

Aroma drifts like a quirky tease,
A blend of pine and some old cheese.
Nature's pantry spills its secrets free,
A fragrant joke just for you and me.

The flowers giggle, peeking below,
At the ants in suits, they steal the show.
In this wild comedy, we all play along,
Where laughter grows and nothing feels wrong.

Sylvan Simplicity

In the woods where squirrels play,
A chipmunk tries to steal my hay.
He wiggles, jigs, and makes a fuss,
While I'm just here, enjoying us.

The trees are tall, the shadows long,
A raccoon sings a silly song.
With branches swaying to the beat,
Nature's rhythm can't be beat.

Beneath the boughs, they dance and leap,
While I just try not to fall asleep.
It's quite a sight, this woodland crew,
A comedy show, for just us two.

So grab a snack, let laughter flow,
In this green world, we steal the show.
Where every leaf tells a joke so grand,
Life can be silly, just as we planned.

Crease of the Bark

In the cracks of tree-wood skin,
Lie secrets where the beetles win.
They march around with such a flair,
As if they're headed to a fair.

A woodpecker taps a laugh or two,
Dressed in colors, bright and new.
He knocks and knocks, oh what a ruckus,
Cracking jokes with each pick-up!

The mushrooms giggle on the ground,
As tiny fairies dance around.
Each crease in bark, a tale to share,
Of woodland life, beyond compare.

So wander here with heart so light,
In creases deep, there's pure delight.
Among the branches, we can play,
And share our laughter every day.

Memories in the Underbrush

Beneath the bramble, tales are spun,
Of critters plotting in the sun.
A rabbit hops with style so sly,
While toads chorus 'Oh my, oh my!'

The underbrush holds laughter near,
As whispers dance on paths we steer.
It's where the wild things find their glee,
A hidden stage, for you and me.

With each tall fern, a joke is told,
Of ants in suits, so brave and bold.
The laughter echoes in the glade,
Where woodland dreams are softly made.

So let us stroll through leafy lanes,
Where humor lives and never wanes.
In this wild place, both free and bright,
We'll weave our stories, pure delight.

Heartwood Whispers

The heart of every tree does speak,
Of woodland friends who play hide and sneak.
A grinning raccoon tags along,
While foxes join in with a song.

Between the roots, the echoes flow,
Of giggling owls who steal the show.
With every rustle, laughter stirs,
In cozy nooks where joy occurs.

The mushrooms twirl with painted glee,
Inviting all to join the spree.
Each hearty laugh, a soft embrace,
In heartwood laughter, we find our place.

So here we sit, beneath green spires,
With woodland wonders and playful fires.
Together we'll weave our bright designs,
In nature's heart where humor shines.

Whispers of Evergreen

In the woods where all the trees,
Chatter softly with the breeze.
A squirrel jokes, a bird will sing,
Nature's laughter is the thing.

Mossy beds are quite the sight,
Holding secrets, sheer delight.
Woodpeckers gossip, oh so loud,
Creating chaos, proud and proud.

The branches wave, oh what a tease,
Like dancers in the autumn breeze.
They poke and prod, those leafy pals,
Stirring giggles, making jests, with gales.

With every rustle, every cheer,
The forest giggles, loud and clear.
So venture forth, take off that frown,
In the greenwood, joy is found!

Fragrant Shadows

In the glade where scents collide,
The gnomes hold court, they take pride.
Mushrooms giggle, grass is green,
Nature's party, quite the scene!

Bees are buzzing comedy acts,
Dancing 'round with sweet contract.
While ants parade in lines, absurd,
Making sure their plans are heard.

Whispers linger in the air,
As pinecone puppets dance with flair.
Furry critters toss a prank,
In melodrama, never blank!

Here in shadows, jocund glow,
This forest knows how fun can grow.
So linger longer, laugh some more,
In fragrant hideouts, joy will soar!

The Forest's Breath

The trees exhale a ticklish breeze,
Caressing branches, oh what tease.
Frogs croak songs, if you can hear,
Chirping jokes, they've got no fear!

The bushes rustle, whispers spread,
Tales of mischief, laughter bred.
A rabbit hops, a turtle grins,
In the embrace of leafy sins.

With twinkling lights, the fireflies dance,
Holding a party, not by chance.
Each flicker sparkles, teasing night,
Nature's jesters, full of light!

Among the boughs, the chuckles burst,
In every nook, it's fun, we thirst.
So grab a seat 'neath leafy roofs,
And join the chorus of playful hoots!

Aromatic Journeys

Let's venture forth to woods so grand,
Where scented trails lie, unplanned.
With laughter trailing, we will roam,
Under canopies we call home.

The flowers wear their fragrant hats,
As busy critters dance like cats.
A picnic here, with honey drips,
As giggles echo from our lips.

Sniffing pine with comical flair,
As if the trees are in a dare.
Each fragrant step, a comedic plot,
Where every misstep is forgot.

So hike along, let spirits lift,
In aromatic laughs, we drift.
With nature's humor all around,
Join the frolic, joy is found!

Canopy Chronicles

In the trees, squirrels play,
Chasing each other, hooray!
One trips and lands on a branch,
A funny move, what a chance!

Birds chirp jokes from up high,
While bees buzz by and sigh.
A woodpecker's tap is a beat,
Dancing ants bring the heat!

Leaves rustle with secrets to share,
Whispers floating through the air.
A raccoon tries on a hat,
Oh, what a fashionable brat!

Nature laughs under the sun,
With silly antics, oh what fun!
Under this great leafy dome,
We find laughter feels like home.

Between the Trees

Along the path, shadows prance,
Branches sway in a wild dance.
A turtle thinks it can keep pace,
But leaves fall down, oh what a race!

Chipmunks have their acorn stash,
But oh, how quickly they crash!
Rolling down in a furry slide,
With giggles echoing far and wide!

Dancing fungi in a line,
Mushrooms try to form a vine.
But they trip on roots all day,
With fungi slipping, what a display!

Sunlight tickles shafts of green,
Nature's laugh, not yet seen.
A breeze brings more jests and glee,
Who knew trees could be so zany?

The Lyrics of the Leaves

Leaves sing softly in the breeze,
But when they giggle, watch the trees!
One rustles loudly, that's not fair,
Pinecone splats with flair everywhere!

A crow croaks out a silly song,
While the shy owl joins along.
Together they start quite a show,
A duet with quite the flow!

Grasshoppers play their wild tunes,
Bouncing under the playful moons.
Yet one gets stuck in a leaf's clutch,
Yelling out, "I need a touch!"

The whispers of the forest frame,
Each joke leaves us with a name.
A serenade that can't be beat,
Where laughter and nature meet!

Breath of the Wild

In deep woods, a breeze runs free,
Tickling all who dare to see.
Trees sway and giggles flicker,
A critter fails—oh, what a sticker!

Barking dogs chase tails in fun,
While frogs leap out, think they've won.
A raccoon sneezes, oh what a sound,
Nature's comedy knows no bound!

Twigs snap under frolicking paws,
Everyone laughs without pause.
The wind whispers ticklish plans,
As laughter spills from nature's hands!

Here in the wild, jesters roam,
Under leaves, they call it home.
With every gust, a chuckle flows,
In this place where hilarity grows!

Coniferous Dreams

In the forest, trees take naps,
Swaying gently, like silly chaps.
A squirrel spins a wild old tale,
While owls hoot, they rarely fail.

The branches stretch, doing yoga moves,
Bending low, in their groovy grooves.
Colors blend, a vibrant mess,
Nature's party, no need to stress.

Whispering Pines

Here they murmur, secrets abound,
Branches gossip without a sound.
Critters chuckle beneath their boughs,
Shushing each other, like silly cows.

The needles tickle, they catch a breeze,
Even the bark laughs with such ease.
Chirping birds drop puns so sweet,
A woodland comedy, can't be beat!

Nature's Ink

With needles dipped in forest ink,
They write of squirrels, and make you think.
A cheeky rabbit hops by with flair,
Jotting down jokes for all to share.

The breeze whispers tales of old,
Of trolls, and gnomes, both brave and bold.
On the pages of the woodland floor,
Laughter echoes forevermore.

Trails of Scented Shadows

Follow the trails of fragrant fun,
Where shadows dance and we all run.
The mushrooms giggle in their small beds,
While ants march on, bumping their heads.

Whiskered snouts and whisked away time,
Nature's laughter is quite sublime.
Each twist and turn is full of jest,
In this woodland, we're truly blessed.

Ciphers in the Conifers

Amid the trees, they whisper sweet,
Like secrets shared in woody heat.
The squirrels giggle, they know the code,
In these tall towers, mischief flowed.

Branches twist in hilarious style,
Each knot a grin, each bend a smile.
They laugh at the breeze that tousles their hair,
As pinecones drop, they dance without a care.

The shadows stretch, creating a play,
A game of tag in the light of day.
With every rustle, a chuckle roams,
Among the trunks, they make their homes.

In this forest of jest, the air is bright,
Where trees and creatures share delight.
The ciphers written on the bark,
Reveal the humor hidden in the dark.

Echoes of the Timberland

Rustling leaves share a punchline bold,
With echoes of laughter, their stories told.
The owls hoot jokes on a moonlit night,
In the timberland, everything feels right.

The timber creaks like a comic's line,
As branches sway, they dance and twine.
Beneath the stars, the deer assemble,
To giggle at shadows, their sides tremble.

A woodpecker with a beak like a quill,
Knocks out rhythms that give a thrill.
The echoes bounce in a funny refrain,
In the heart of timberland, joy does reign.

So come and listen to the forest's glee,
Where every rustle is a cue to be free.
In echoes and laughter, this place unfolds,
A tapestry of humor that never gets old.

The Softness of the Shadows

Beneath the boughs where shadows play,
Everything seems to giggle away.
The sunbeams slip through the leafy dance,
And everything finds a funny chance.

A caterpillar with a dream so grand,
Wants to be a butterfly, not a bland.
He dresses up, all silly and bright,
In a coat of leaves, what a sight!

The shadows whisper their softest jest,
As creatures lounge in their leafy nest.
A raccoon slips, and oh what a fall,
The forest erupts in laughter, a free-for-all!

In this world of whimsy and delight,
Where shadows giggle in the golden light,
Find the humor where the soft winds blow,
In the heart of the woods, let the laughter grow.

Dreams in Green

In a world where every branch can sing,
With visions bright, what joy they bring.
The ferns wear crowns of emerald hue,
While the flowers giggle in laughter too.

A raccoon dreams of sushi delight,
While the fireflies twinkle in the night.
In the meadow, they hold a feast,
With bugs and blooms, a jolly beast.

The trees murmur tales of days gone by,
With humorous twists that make one sigh.
Where dreams in green dance on the breeze,
And laughter echoes through the leaves with ease.

So venture forth to this quirky land,
Where everything silly is close at hand.
In dreams woven thick, with humor's embrace,
Find joy in the green, this enchanting place.

Sprouts of Inspiration

In the shade, I wrote a tale,
Of trees that danced, not swayed or pale.
A squirrel critiqued, with a twitch of its tail,
While birds sang melodies that never fail.

I pondered words, then lost my place,
As woodpeckers chuckled, a feathery race.
I thought of rhymes, oh what a disgrace,
When frog choirs croaked, they took up the space.

A breeze breezed in, wearing a grin,
Telling me jokes that made my head spin.
With every new laugh, I felt the kin,
Of critters in woodland, where fun won't thin.

So if you seek wisdom, heed this song,
The woods are silly, where we all belong.
Grab a pencil, join in—come along!
For inspiration's waiting, never wrong.

Seasons of the Scented Forest

In spring, the flowers tried to make a show,
While rabbits bickered over where to grow.
The sun just giggled, 'Don't steal their glow!'
As bees buzzed by, shouting, 'Take it slow!'

Summer brought warmth, and lizards got bold,
They lounged in sunbeams, wearing shades, so old.
They swapped tall tales of adventures untold,
While ants formed lines, their stories were sold.

When autumn arrived, leaves stuck out their tongue,
Falling in rhythm, like songs that we sung.
Squirrels were busy, lived life young and hung,
While acorns whispered, "Join in, stay among!"

Winter rolled in, with a cap and a scarf,
Snowflakes teased branches, a chilly giraffe.
Yet laughter still echoed, through every path,
For even in frost, there's always a laugh.

Whispers of the Woods

A breeze soared high, with secrets to share,
The trees stood tall, with a mighty flair.
'What's that, old oak?' said the birch with a stare,
'Oh nothing, just gossip, don't you despair!'

The stumps chipped in, with a snicker or two,
'We've seen a few things, oh yes, it's true!
Like a fox in boots, who thought he could skew,
A dance party for mushrooms—what a view!'

Mice played charades in the roots of the ground,
While frogs composed songs, all slightly unbound.
A raccoon stepped up, sharing laughter around,
'You think your tales are funny? Mine astound!'

So the woods filled with whispers, in every nook,
Of giggles and joy, every creature's book.
Join the fun, come take a look,
For nature's odd stories are worth a hook.

The Green Veil of Memory

I wandered through dreams, where green shadows danced,

The trees shared jokes, like children entranced.
With laughter like echoes, as if they had pranced,
And flowers chimed in, as if they had chanced.

Old Pine stood tall, with a twinkle and wink,
'Time's just a jest, don't you overthink!'
Nearby, a chipmunk sipped water to drink,
And pondered all truths with a mischievous blink.

I laughed at the sight, with tales to unwind,
Of woodland creatures, both clever and kind.
With memories blooming, I hoped to remind,
Life is a tale, and laughter's well-defined.

So gather the joy, let the past's petals fall,
In the green-tinged woods, where the giggles call.
For every old story's a chance for us all,
To weave our own fabric, let laughter be tall.

Cradle of Conifers

In the woods where trees confide,
Laughter dances, like a ride.
Needles tickle, branches sway,
Witty whispers greet the day.

Squirrels plotting, nuts in tow,
Jokes exchanged, a forest show.
There's a gnome with silly hats,
Chasing shadows, dodging rats.

Tall trunks stand and roll their eyes,
As raccoons craft their alibis.
So gather round, it's time to quiz,
Who wrote that joke? A tree? Who is?

With every gust, a giggle grows,
Nature's jest - anything goes!
The conifers will crack a grin,
Amidst the woodsy tales we spin.

Nature's Ink

In the meadow, thoughts take flight,
Crickets chirp with sheer delight.
A quill made from a willow's sway,
Nature writes in funnies, hey!

Fragrant blooms with puns galore,
Dandelions giggle, wanting more.
Bee hives buzzing, plotting schemes,
Ink from nectar, fueled by dreams.

Mushrooms sing, a spore-filled choir,
Underneath, the ants conspire.
Scribbled thoughts in shades of green,
Nature's humor, truly seen.

A deer prances with flair so bold,
Perhaps it's tickled from stories told.
The forest's laughter never shrinks,
It's nature's ink, full of winks.

The Aroma of Solitude

In solitude, a scent unfolds,
Whiffs of laughter near the folds.
A cedar couch, a pinewood chair,
Each whiff's a chuckle in the air.

Quiet moments filled with cheer,
Echoes of humor, crystal clear.
The breeze carries tales of jest,
Nature giggles, life's the best!

Mossy carpets, soft and vast,
Whisper secrets of the past.
A skunk serenades with style,
Leaving us to laugh a while.

So linger long where scents collide,
In solitude, let laughter ride.
The essence of the great outdoors,
Keeps us chuckling, like before.

Forest Footprints

Footprints mark a playful race,
Bounding bunnies, such a chase!
Every step leaves room for glee,
Nature's path, so wild and free.

Bears with boots on just for fun,
Waddling like they've just begun.
Deer in sneakers strut with pride,
As squirrels giggle, cannot hide.

Castaway shoes from years gone past,
Stories hidden, laughter vast.
Every print a tale to tell,
In the woods, we all know well.

So step with joy upon the ground,
In nature's dance, let luck be found.
A footprint here, a snicker there,
The forest smiles, a merry air.

Harmony of the Pines

In the forest, trees do sway,
Yet one stood still, locking the play.
Squirrels dart, their nuts go lost,
The wise old trunk just laughs at the cost.

Birds sing tunes that make no sense,
A crow joins in, a minor offense.
The branches shake with giggles loud,
As the acorns tumble, feeling proud.

A deer prances by, with hooves so light,
Trips on roots, what a humorous sight!
Trees chuckle low, their barks untold,
Nature's jesters, both timeless and bold.

So come take a stroll, join the cheer,
Where laughter echoes, and worries disappear.
Under the canopy, take a chance,
In the realm of the trees, let's all dance!

A Whispering Canopy

The leaves above whisper secrets sly,
As squirrels plot their nut heist high.
With acorns rolling, oh what a scene,
A forest giggle, so fresh and green.

A chipmunk pops out, dressed in fur,
As if he's off to a great big spur!
The wind teases, "Where's your coat?"
He shrugs, "I'm warm, like a boat afloat!"

Rabbits hop by, with a skip and a twirl,
"Why the rush?" asks a ladybug girl.
"Running late for a hoppy affair,"
She giggles and darts, without a care.

Under this vast, whispering dome,
The humor of nature feels just like home.
So take a break, breathe in the fun,
And let the laughter under trees run!

Tales from the Treetops

Above the world, where the eagles soar,
A raccoon reads, "What's this tree lore?"
He turns the pages, upside down,
"What's this nonsense? I need a crown!"

A woodpecker knocks, "You've got it wrong!
These stories are funky, let's sing a song!"
With branches swaying, they form a band,
The hollow logs echo, oh, isn't it grand?

Each tale unfolds in a humor-filled jest,
The squirrels share who's the very best nest!
While the owls hoot with wise, gruff glee,
"Find me a laugh, just sit, you'll see."

So gather 'round, let laughter rise,
In the treetops, under open skies.
Where stories weave, and nature flies,
Join the fun, let your spirit rise!

Fleeting Footfalls in the Forest

Pat pat pat, what's that sound?
A rabbit escapes with a dramatic bound!
He thought he'd sneak, oh what a mistake,
The leaves snickered as he hit the lake.

A fox joins in on this merry chase,
"Can't catch me, I'm too full of grace!"
But tripped on a twig, did a silly roll,
The forest roared, "What a great goal!"

Mice scamper quick, playing hide and seek,
"Think we've lost them?" "Not if they squeak!"
A chipmunk laughs, "Look who's in the mud!"
As the raccoons slide, creating a thud.

These fleeting footfalls, a joyful race,
In the forest's embrace, there's always a place.
To laugh till dusk, to bounce and play,
Where every misstep brightens the day!

Boughs of Memory

Underneath the towering trees,
Squirrels hold their nutty glee.
Branches bend with joy and cheer,
Whispers float, but who's to hear?

Laughter rides the gusty gale,
Swinging from a leafy trail.
Every pine cone tells a joke,
As I sip my iced oak smoke.

Jumping jays with sass aplenty,
Mocking all—it's quite a frenzy!
Boughs bend low, in secret chat,
While woodland critters tip their hat.

Memory whirls in fragrant haze,
Dancing through the sunlit maze.
A forest floor of silly dance,
Where thoughts take root, given a chance.

Essence of the Canopy

In the shade where shadows weave,
Chirpy bugs don't dare to leave.
Up above, the branches sway,
Making sure they're bright all day.

A wacky crow drops jokes like seeds,
While ferns discuss their ancient deeds.
The air's a blend of green and fun,
With every heartbeat under the sun.

Streams of laughter, leaves of green,
Mirthful sights can be seen.
Sassy owls with peepers wide,
Join the joke parade with pride.

Canopy's embrace is bold,
While squirrel antics never get old.
A ticklish breeze—the perfect score,
Here, nobody can be a bore.

Verdant Reveries

In a glade where giggles grow,
Frogs in bow ties steal the show.
Bright-eyed fawns with leaps and bounds,
Join in on the froggie sounds.

Each leaf whispers a secret song,
Nature's revels all day long.
Sticks play drums that echo loud,
As flowers sway and laugh, so proud.

Mushrooms wear their happy caps,
Bouncing to the beat, perhaps!
Harmonies of rustling green,
In this whimsical, wild scene.

Dreams weave tight like tree trunks strong,
In this verdant land where I belong.
A sway, a laugh—a world so bright,
Here, every moment feels just right.

A Symphony of Needles

Twirling in a dance sublime,
Needles tap in perfect rhyme.
Trees adorned in emerald flair,
Laugh away without a care.

Whispers crawl through needle beds,
As critters giggle with their threads.
In this chorus, life's a breeze,
Even ants can jam with ease.

Bees buzzing in a funky tune,
Chasing shadows past the moon.
Echoes ripple through the night,
In this forest, hearts take flight.

A symphony with every step,
Nature's jesters, oh so adept.
With every slice of merry sound,
In the green, laughter's found.

Solace Among the Pines

In the woods, I found my bliss,
A squirrel tried to steal a kiss.
The branches giggled, swayed and waved,
While I just stood there, slightly flayed.

The breeze was cheeky, made me sneeze,
It teased my hair and ruffled leaves.
A chorus of laughter in every crack,
I swear, those trees were plotting a snack.

My picnic spread, all laid with care,
But ants arrived, oh such a scare!
They danced in circles, a wild ballet,
I chuckled as I watched the buffet.

Among the pines, I laughed with glee,
Nature's jesters and silly spree.
With every rustle, a new surprise,
The forest shared its goofy guise.

Laughter in the Needles

The needles whisper, secrets slight,
A raccoon winks, what a sight!
With each soft step, a crackle sings,
Underfoot, the humor springs.

The sunbeam's tickle makes shadows dance,
While a chipmunk gives me a playful glance.
It scurries up, then down, then back,
In its own little world, a comic act.

I tossed a snack, aimed for a treat,
But hit a tree instead, oh what a feat!
The laughter echoed, a forest song,
Bearing witness to where I went wrong.

In this woodland, folly reigns supreme,
Where pine trees giggle, and laughter beams.
Even the skies seem to chuckle bright,
In this comedy show, all feels right.

Fragrant Footprints

With every step, a whiff of cheer,
The forest smiles, bringing near.
A trail of giggles under my feet,
As nature's aroma makes my day sweet.

I try to dance, misstep in glee,
While bees buzz by, as if to agree.
A cutie bunny hops right along,
Quirky joins in with its own little song.

The laughter of leaves in the faintest breeze,
Makes every stumble feel like a tease.
With fragrant footprints, I prance and twirl,
In this scented realm, life's a whirl.

So, bring on the laughter, leave worries behind,
In these fragrant footsteps, joy's easy to find.
With every aroma, a chuckle ignites,
In the heart of the woods, laughter delights.

Reflections of the Tall Ones

Among the giants, stories unfold,
With bark as wise and laughter bold.
They lean in closely, sharing tales,
Of squirrels and winds, and epic fails.

A tree stump chuckled, 'I've seen it all,'
As I tripped over my laces and fell.
The roots burst out, in fits of mirth,
These tall ones declare, 'We know your worth!'

Each knotted branch, a witness to life,
Holding our joys and laughter rife.
They sway above, in a breezy play,
Dancing to tunes of the light-hearted day.

So here I stand, with the wise and tall,
In this forest, where giggles enthrall.
Every reflection, every bough and spin,
Rings of laughter, where joy begins.

The Lure of the Lonely Path

In the woods where whispers play,
Leaves dance in a shimmery display.
I took a stroll without a map,
And ended up in a squirrel's lap.

They offered me a nut or two,
Said, 'We're the locals, who are you?'
I chuckled at their furry flair,
And joined their acorn-eating affair.

Needle and Quill

A needle fell from a sewing spree,
'How sharp!' it laughed, 'Come dance with me!'
The quill retorted with a scribbly grin,
'I'll write you a tale, let's begin!'

Together they crafted a stylish thread,
A story of thimbles that went to bed.
In dreams, they dashed through fabric fields,
Sewing up laughter, their joy yields.

Forest Lullabies

The trees hummed tunes to the buzzing bees,
While rabbits waltzed with the gentle breeze.
A fox crooned softly with a feather hat,
And all around, the mushrooms clapped.

With every note, a giggle grew,
As owls wore glasses and played peekaboo.
A song of sprightly, carefree cheer,
Echoed through branches, far and near.

Notes from the Saplings

Young saplings scribbled in the dirt,
'Why are the acorns wearing a skirt?'
A wise old tree chuckled with glee,
'It's a fancy dress party, can't you see?'

'Oops!' cried a twig, 'I'm underdressed!'
While a beetle struts, feeling quite blessed.
These notes of mischief, sweet and sly,
Made the forest twirl as the night drifts by.

Evergreen Meditations

Amidst the trees, I sit and think,
About the time I spilled my drink.
A squirrel watched me in surprise,
As laughter danced in those bright eyes.

With needles sharp and bark so rough,
I ponder life, so weird and tough.
Nature chuckles, breezy and free,
At my missteps beneath the tree.

The branches sway, they poke and tease,
While birds conspire to steal my cheese.
In whispers sweet, the leaves conspire,
To make me laugh, oh what a choir!

So here I dwell, in shade and glee,
Nature's humor delights me.
With every rustle, every sigh,
The forest jokes as time goes by.

A Breath of the Wild

In wilds where laughter loves to dwell,
I found a skunk with quite a smell.
He winked at me, or maybe squinted,
And I just laughed, completely minted.

The breeze was light, and so was I,
As I chased a butterfly on high.
But tripped on roots that sneaky grabbed,
Oh, how the forest truly blabbed!

A deer peered in, said, "What a show!"
With berries stuck in her furry bow.
I blushed in nature's comic light,
As giggles rang till the fall of night.

A breath of wild is not so grim,
Where clumsy fools can laugh on whim.
In greenery, where joy abounds,
Life's funny tricks are all around.

Cedar Shakes and Sonnets

In cedar groves, I wrote a rhyme,
About a squirrel who danced with time.
He twirled around with such great flair,
While I just sat in my comfy chair.

The trees chimed in with creaks and croaks,
As whispers shared some whimsical jokes.
I threw a nut, it flew so far,
And hit a stump, a pine-shaped star!

Oh, woodland muses, how you jest,
With every shake, you tease the best.
From acorns plump to branches bare,
Each moment's laughter fills the air.

With every sonnet, let's embrace,
The joy found in this wild, green space.
In playful prose where laughter stays,
Cedar shakes will always amaze.

Boughs of Imagination

Under boughs where daydreams play,
A raccoon winks, 'Come join my fray!'
He sips from a mug labeled 'Nature',
With antics bold, he's quite the feature.

The sun tickles leaves; they chuckle too,
As I, perplexed, just watch the view.
My imagination takes a flight,
As trees burst forth with sheer delight!

A chipmunk jives in rhythm so tight,
While shadows dance in the golden light.
With each rustle and glance they share,
Life's amusing hints float through the air.

In this wild world, I'm never alone,
Where laughter breeds and joy is grown.
Boughs of whimsy twist and shout,
In nature's spin, there's never doubt.

Musings in the Mist

In the forest, thoughts take flight,
Trees giggle in morning light.
A squirrel stole my sandwich fast,
Now I question my breakfast past.

Leaves whisper secrets, oh so sweet,
While mushrooms dance beneath my feet.
A raccoon peeks with mischief in mind,
Grinning wide, he's one of a kind.

Fog plays tricks, hides my boots,
Nature's jest with tree-like roots.
I swear I heard a twig laugh loud,
Echoing joy among the crowd.

As I wander, the ferns agree,
Life's a jolly mystery.
With every step, new stories spring,
In this forest, joy takes wing.

Secrets of the Sylvan

The trees are gossiping, oh so sly,
Why did the owl let out a cry?
Said he saw a bear in bright pink socks,
Chasing shadows, hiding in rocks.

A fox in a hat, he struts with pride,
While chipmunks giggle and slide aside.
They plot a party, leaves for décor,
Inviting critters from forest and more.

Mushrooms wear capes, the scene is set,
Dancing under stars, no sign of regret.
A hedgehog in shades, leaning back,
Tells tales of the home in his cozy pack.

Laughter sparkles in every glade,
As woodland friends join the parade.
Secrets shared among the trees,
Embrace the humor in the breeze.

Under the Canopy of Stars

Underneath the twinkling glow,
I tripped on roots, feeling quite slow.
A raccoon snickered; I stumbled high,
Waving my arms like I could fly.

Crickets chirp with perfect timing,
While fireflies dance, light all-climbing.
A bear reads poetry, makes me chuckle,
In this night, we all snuggle.

A badger drapes himself in style,
Wearing a moonbeam, just for a while.
Soft laughter echoes through the night,
As woodland critters take to flight.

Stars drop secrets, bright and bold,
Each a story waiting to be told.
Under the canopy, we're all friends,
In nature's jest, joy never ends.

The Scent of Ancient Echoes

Whispers of the old trees linger,
Raccoons plot with a flick of their finger.
Echos of laughter float through the air,
A chipmunk's jokes, surprisingly rare.

Roots twist and turn like tongue-tied jokes,
As owls wink and share their pokes.
A bear with a hat sits sipping tea,
Chatting with shadows, quite carefree.

Acorns fall like laughter galore,
Squirrels tumble, they want more!
With every giggle, the forest throbs,
Crafting whimsy, as nature robs.

Ancient trees hum a funny tune,
Under the glow of a cheeky moon.
With echoes of mirth, the night takes flight,
In the woods, everything feels just right.

Scented Reverberations

In the forest, the trees wear a grin,
Their aroma dances, where fun begins.
Squirrels are prancing, with nuts in their paws,
While birds chirp jokes, breaking nature's laws.

A whiff of the breeze tickles my nose,
Like a pie cooling down, it just glows.
I giggle at shadows that creep and crawl,
Conspiring with critters to prank us all.

Each branch has a story that's tall as can be,
Of mischief and laughter, wild and free.
With dappled sunlight that twinkles and beams,
We weave through the scents, lost in our dreams.

So, breathe in the chuckles, let silliness flow,
In this fragrant realm where the heart can glow.
Let every inhale be flavored with glee,
A comedy taught by the wise old tree.

A Tapestry of Fragrance

In a meadow of green, where the aromas mix,
The flowers tell stories, I'm here for the tricks.
Petals wear smiles — they know what's in store,
With every sweet whiff, I can't help but roar.

Bumbles buzz by with a laugh and a wink,
Reminding me not to take life on the brink.
The breeze hugs my cheeks, gives a playful tease,
While leaves play the fiddle to the tune of the trees.

As I frolic through patches of silly delight,
A sprinkle of humor dances in the light.
Whiffs of good fortune float soft on the wind,
It's a fragrant adventure, where laughter's a friend.

So let's gather the scents, in colors they burst,
A tapestry woven, where giggles come first.
In this fragrant wonder, let joy lead the way,
With every sweet inhale, let's dance and play.

Echoes Among the Firs

Among the tall giants, I hear echoes loud,
Of laughter and lightness, they make me so proud.
Branches are gossiping, what's that they've heard?
Of jests made by critters, I'm wildly disturbed!

The needles sway softly, giving high-fives,
While shadows bounce lightly, they all seem alive.
A chipmunk in costume is leading the show,
With jokes that tumble, like leaves in a flow.

The air feels like candy, both sweet and absurd,
Each breeze carries laughter, no need for a word.
In this forest of echoes, the humor runs free,
As the firs join the chorus, all merry with glee.

So let's skip through the whispers, unshackle the fun,
With nature as comic, we'll laugh till we're done.
In this jolly old forest, our spirits take flight,
Among the tall whispers, we dance with delight.

Serene Saplings

In a garden of giggles, where seedlings sprout,
Tiny trees whisper secrets, they can't live without.
With roots in the humor, they stretch for the skies,
Bubbling with laughter, oh, what a surprise!

Each sapling a jester, on nature's big stage,
With wigs made of moss and a sappy old page.
As raindrops tickle, they chuckle and sway,
Telling you tales in their own sprightly way.

The sun beams down warmly, it joins in the fun,
Bouncing on branches, till the day is done.
With petals like confetti, they dance all about,
In this serene haven, old worries fade out.

So come join the frolic, beneath bows so low,
With each fragrant moment, let mirth overflow.
In this charming abode, where laughter abounds,
Serene saplings giggle, in joy they are found.

www.ingramcontent.com/pod-product-compliance
Lightning Source LLC
Chambersburg PA
CBHW071822160426
43209CB00003B/165